A Student Investment Learning Guide

Understanding the Mathematics of Investment
Concepts and its Principles

Celicia Lee
MP Publishing

Copyright

© 2018 by Celicia Lee

All rights reserved. This book or any portion thereof may not be reproduced or used in any manner whatsoever without the express written permission of the publisher except for the use of brief quotations in a book review.

Table of Contents

INTRODUCTION 5

PART ONE 7

SIMPLE INTEREST 7

WHAT IS INTEREST AND HOW DOES IT WORK? 7
ELEMENTS OF INTEREST COMPUTATION 9
GUIDELINES IN MEASURING TIME 12
METHODS OF COMPUTING INTEREST 19
GUIDELINES IN CONVERTING TIME 21

PART TWO 23

DISCOUNT 23

PART THREE 35

COMPOUND INTEREST 35

NATURE OF COMPOUND INTEREST 35
COMPOUND INTEREST 35
PRESENT VALUE OF A COMPOUND AMOUNT 41
PRESENT VALUE WITH FRACTIONAL INTEREST PERIOD 43
FINDING THE INTEREST RATE 44

FINDING THE TIME 48
RELATIONSHIP BETWEEN NOMINAL AND EFFECTIVE RATES 50

BONUS KNOWLEDGE 53

Introduction

Most students are intimidated by mathematics not because they dislike mathematical operations and signs, but because they do not understand the basic premise of what they are solving. In many instances, they simply memorize the different mathematical formulas, but they can barely explain the meaning of their anal answer.

The mathematics of investment is not limited to those who are in the banking sector or in the business industry. It applies to everyone and affects the daily activities of people from different walks of life. Borrowing or lending of money, buying household appliances on cash or instalment basis, depositing money in a bank, and purchasing farm machinery all entail investment principles, as well as other activities that involve buying and selling shares of stocks and bonds.

Each chapter outlines specific learning objectives and contains a review to guide and check the learning and degree of comprehension of the students or teachers to use.

PART ONE

SIMPLE INTEREST

What is Interest and how does it work?

Interest refers to the amount paid for the use of money or the price paid for the use of credit. For example, if Scarlett borrows money from Horizon Bank, the will be charged with Interest by the bank on account of the borrowed money. Interest may also be viewed as income; it refers to the amount received as a result of the possession or ownership of a contractual obligation to pay on the part of another. Thus, in the case of Horizon Bank, the interest paid by Scarlett upon maturity of the loan is treated as Income. This generally arises because of the use of money or credit. On the part of the owner of money or lender of credit. It is viewed as income. On the other hand, it is treated as an expense by the user of money or credit.

Interest also serves as a mechanism of imposing penalty to a borrower for not paying a matured financial obligation at a specified time. For example, on March 1, 2016, Debbie bought a set of home appliances from Hudson's Mann Appliance Center, which is payable after 6 months. If Debbie cannot pay the full amount on its maturity date, she will be penalized in the form of an interest.

Interest, therefore, comes from certain transactions which are economic or financial in character. A transaction is considered economic or financial in character if there is monetary value involved in the exchange. The economic transaction of Scarlett from the above example is the borrowing of money, while that of Debbie is the buying of goods or properties on account.

Moreover, there are two parties in a transaction involving payment of interest: the lender or creditor and the borrower or debtor. Lender or creditor refers to the party lending money or extending credit. He/She expects to earn income from this transaction. The borrower or debtor, meanwhile refers to the party using the money or credit, who expects future expenses as the cost of using it. When money is deposited in the bank for safekeeping, the depositor is considered as the creditor and the bank is viewed as the party obliged to pay the interest.

From the first example above, Scarlett is the borrower and Horizon Bank serves as the lender, while the second Debbie is the debtor Hudson's Mann Appliance Center acts as the creditor.

Elements of Interest Computation

The amount of interest that a lender receives or a borrower pays is computed using the following elements:
1. Principal
2. Interest rate
3. Time

Principal refers to the amount of money extended for the credit or the money deposited in the bank for safekeeping.

Interest rate refers to the charged amount for using the money over a certain period. It is expressed in percent, but is usually converted to decimal for ease in the computation process. Unless otherwise indicated in the problem, the interest rate is expressed in percent per year.

Time refers to the period covered from the time that the money (principal) is borrowed until its due date. The due date for the payment of the principal is known as the maturity date. The reference point of time is 1 year or 12 months.

Simple Interest Computation

Simple interest refers to an interest that is computed only once from the time the amount is borrowed until it is paid. In other words, there is only one interest payment made during the entire period of borrowing. Under the concept of simple interest, the amount of interest is usually paid at the maturity date or due date.

The formula to compute the sample interest is as follows:

Interest = Principal x Rate x Time

Or: I = PRT

Where :

I = Interest

P = Principal

R : Rate

T = Time

Finding the Principal
In some instances, the simple interest (I), the rate (R), and the time (T) are given, but the principal amount (P) is unknown. The principal amount can be determined by simply manipulating the basic formula.
The principal is computed as follows:
P = I /RT

Finding the Rate
In some instances rate (R) is not given in simple interest computation and the data on the principal (P), the interest paid (I), and the time (T) are provided, the rate of interest is computed as follows:
R = I /PT

Finding the Time
When time (T) is unknown and the principal (P), the rate (R), and the interest (I) are provided, the time (T) is computed as follows:
T = I /PR

Maturity Value or Amount

Maturity value or amount refers to the sum of the principal and interest. It is the future value of the principal amount, expressed in the following formula :

M=P+I

where:

M = Maturity value

P = Principal

I = Interest

By expanding the basic simple interest formula, the maturity value is computed using the following formula:

M = P+PRT

By the process of factoring, maturity value can be expressed as:

M = P (1 + RT)

Guidelines in Measuring Time

The following simple guidelines may be observed in measuring time.

1. If the time stated in the problem is expressed in number of days, the year should be likewise be measured in days. There are two methods of measuring the year in terms of the number of days. These are :

a. Ordinary interest

b. Exact interest

These two methods will be discussed further in the succeeding topic in this chapter.

2. Unless otherwise specified, it is assumed that both the loan date and the maturity date are on the same year.

For example, Josephine borrowed $ 10,000 on January 2, and the loam matures on May 30. 2012. Since the loan date did not mention the year, it is assumed that January 2 refers to January 2, 2012.

3. If the loan date is given and the maturity period is expressed in months, the maturity period date shall coincide with the loan date, regardless of the number of days in each month.

For example, Mr Clarke borrowed $15,000 on May 15, 2012, payable after 6 months. The due date of the loan will be on November 15, 2012, 6 months after the loan date, notwithstanding the number of days in a particular month between May to November.

4. If the loan date and the due date are given in the problem. the number of days between the two given dates

are computed using the exact time method and approximate time method. This is explained further in the succeeding topic in this chapter.

Ordinary and Exam Interest Methods

Ordinary and exact interest methods are the two methods used to determine the interest when the time given in the problem is expressed in number of days but the interest rate is expressed in percent per year.

For example, how much it the interest payable by Mr Smith if he borrows $20,000 at 7%, payable after 250 days?

It can be observed in the given problem that the interest rate is expressed in terms of year, while the period covered is in days. To facilitate an easy computation, the given number of days should be expressed in relation to the total number of days in a year.

Query : Shall we use 360 or 365 days in 1 year?
Answer : It will depend whether the ordinary interest method or the exact interest method is used in computing the amount of interest. Ordinary and exact interest

methods actually determine the denominator used in computing for the time

Ordinary Interest Method

The ordinary method of computing interest uses 360 days in a year. Thus, as the query above-how much it the interest payable by Mr Smith if he borrows $20,000 at 7%, payable after 250 days-the interest, using the ordinary interest method is computed as follows.

I = PRT
=20,000 x 0.07 x 250/360
= P 972.22

Exact Interest Mod

The exact interest method adopts 365 days in a year. But in a leap year, it uses 366 days.

Thus, under the exact interest method, the interest payable by Mr Smith is computed as follows:

I = PRT
= 20,000 x 0.07 x 250/365
= $958.90

Relationship between Ordinary and Exact Interest Methods

It is observable that one difference between ordinary interest and exact methods is the denominator used in the time element of the Interest formula. Another salient difference is that the amount of simple interest using the ordinary interest method is higher compared to exact interest method.

Working on the relationship between the two in terms of days, the ratio of 360 days against 365 days is as follows:

Ratio = 360/365
= 0.986301:1

This means that the exact interest is 0.986301 of the Ordinary interest. Thus, if we multiply the ordinary interest by 0.986301, the result will be the amount of simple interest using the exact interest method.

Using the data in the same illustration, the relationship is as follows:

Exact interest = Ordinary interest x 0.986301
= 972.22 x 0.906301
= $958.90

Conversely, the ratio of 365 days against 360 days is as follows:

Ratio = 365/360

= 1.013889:1

The ordinary interest in 1.013889 of the exact interest. Again, multiplying the exact interest by 1.013889 will give the amount of ample interest under the ordinary interest method.

Hence, using the same data, the relationship is expressed as follows:

Ordinary interest = Exact interest x 1.013889

= 958.90 x 1.013889

= $972.22

Exact Time and Approximate Time

The methods of exact time and approximate time are used to count the number of days in a given period where the loan date and the due dates are mentioned.

For example, Bryan borrowed $20,000 at 8% on March 15, 2012, which in payable on August 20, 2012.

Query: In computing the interest, how many days are there from March 15, 2012 to August 20, 2012?

Answer: The number of days between the two periods will depend if the exact time or approximate time is used.

Exact time and approximate time are two methods used in computing for the numerator in the time element.

Exact or Actual Time Method

In the exact time method, time is determined by adding me number of days of all the months between the loan date and the maturity date.

Thus, there are 158 actual or exact days from March 15, 2013 to August 20, 2012. Computed as follows:

March (31-15) = 16 days
April = 30 days
May = 31 days
June = 30 days
July = 31 days
August = 20 days
Exact time = 158 days

In counting the days within a given period, exclude the first day and include the last day. Thus, March 15 was excluded, but August 20 was included in the count for the problem.

Approximate Time Method

Under the approximate time method, it is assumed that from March 15, 2012 to August 20, 2012 under the approximate time method, computed as follows:

March (30-15) = 15 days
April = 30 days
May = 30 days
June = 30 days
May = 30 days
August = 20 days
Approximate time = 155 days

It can be observed that under the approximate time method, the total number of days for March is 30.

Methods of Computing Interest

When the time given in a simple interest problem is between two dates, there are two methods to compute the days for the numerator and the denominator

To compute the number of days in the numerator, the methods are :

1. Exact or actual time method; and
2. Approximate time method.

Likewise, to compute the days in the denominator, the methods are :
1. Ordinary interest method; and
2. Exact interest method.

In other words, there are four possible combinations to determine the simple interest between to dates.
The four possible combinations and their corresponding formulas are:

1. Ordinary interest method using exact or actual time:
I = P x R x Exact time/ 360

2. Ordinary interest method using approximate time:
I = P x R x Aggroximate time/ 360

3. Exact interest method using exact time:
I = P x R x Exact time / 365

4. Exact interest method using approximate time:
I = P x R x Aggroximate time /365

Guidelines in Converting Time

The time element in simple interest is computed by dividing the interest with the product of the principal and the rate. Sometimes, the result of the computation is a decimal or a whole number and a decimal. The decimal should be converted to days or months.

For example, Romeo is planning to accumulate $50,000 by investing $30,000 at Mini Bank with 12% simple interest per year. How long will it take him to accumulate the $50,000?

The period to accumulate the desired amount can be computed using the formula to find time. It can be deduced that the simple interest in this case is $20,000, taken from the difference between the desired amount of $50,000 and the amount invested of $10,000 at 12% interest per year.

The time is computed as follows:
T = 20,000 /30,000x0.12
= 5.56 years

Therefore, it will take Romeo 5.56 years to accumulate the $50,000. The decimal 0.56 means that it is a fraction of a year or of 12 months. This figure should be expressed in terms of days or months.

PART TWO

DISCOUNT

Nature of Discount

The term "discount," as a noun, can mean any the following:

1. Reduction from the full amount of a price or debt.
2. The interest deducted in advance in lending commercial paper.
3. The rate of interest deducted in a lending transaction.

As a verb, discount may connote the following:
1. To deduct from a price.
2. To advance money after deducting interest.
3. To reduce the value.

Based on the different (temptations given above, discount has no precise and definite meaning, basically, the meaning depends on how it is used on a given context.

By the process of deduction, discount, therefore, refers to the difference between two values and the present value of an amount. We will use these two concepts of discount in the succeeding discussions.

Simple Discount

Simple discount refers to the difference between the future value or amount due and its present value.

Simple discount is also equivalent to the simple interest. It is called simple discount because the discount is computed only once during the entire period of borrowing.

To facilitate my discussion of simple discount, the terms in simple interest are placed beside its equivalent terms in simple discount.

Under Simple Interest =
Under Simple discount
Principal =
I Present value
Maturity value or amount =
Future value or amount due
Interest =
Discount

Interest rate = Discount rate

Query: What is the salient difference between simple interest and simple discount?

Answer: Under the concept of simple interest, the interest is payable on the due date of the loan. In other words, the borrower pays the creditor or the bank the principal amount plus interest on the maturity date. Hence, the borrower receives the full amount on that date.

The Term "To Discount" and the Present Value

The term "to discount" means to determine the present value Of an amount In other words, we are answering the query: What IS the value now (present value) of a certain amount payable at a later period?

Before we go further, let us first recall the concept of maturit'y value of simple interest discussed in Chapter 1 '

The formula to compute for maturity value by the process of factoring is:

$M = P(1 + RT)$

Where:

M = Maturity Value

P = Principal

R = Rate

T = Time

Maturity value refers to the sum of the principal and interest. In other words, it is the future value of the principal at a certain interest rate.

The principal in simple interest then, is equivalent to the present value of maturity value or future amount.

In simple discount, the problem normally states the maturity value. On the other hand, in simple interest computation, the problem states the principal. The procedure applied to compute the principal or present value is reversed when computing for simple interest.

To solve for principal (P) in the above formula, divide both sides of the equation by (1 + RT); hence:

$$\frac{M}{(1+RT)} = \frac{P(1+RT)}{(1+RT)}$$

Cancelling (1 + RT) on the right of the equation, the formula to compute the present value of simple discount appears as follows:

P = M

$(1+RT)$

Bank Discount

Bank discount refers to the amount of interest deducted by the bank in advance. The interest is computed based on the maturity value of the loan. In other words, when the bank discounted a loan, the borrower receives an amount less than what was borrowed, since the interest has been deducted in advance.

Bank discount is computed as follows:

Bank discount = Maturity value x Discount rate x Time

The amount that the borrower receives is called proceeds. It Is the discounted value of the loan, and is computed as follows:

Proceeds = Maturity value - Bank discount

Promissory Notes

A promissory note is a written promise signed by the maker to pay another Person a certain sum of money in a fixed or determinable future time.

The two types of promissory notes are;

1. Simple interest promissory note
2. Discounted interest promissory note

A promissory note may also be:

1. An interest-bearing note
2. A non-interest bearing note

The note is considered interest bearing when a certain interest rate is specified on its face, while a non-interest bearing note does not mention of any interest.

In a simple interest promissory note, the amount that appears on the face of the note is the principal amount. The principal and the interest comprise the total amount payable upon the maturity date. In the discounted interest promissory note, however, the amount that appears on the face of the note is the maturity value of the loan.

The parts of a promissory note are as follows:

1. Maker - the person who signs and executes the note because of borrowing.

2. Payee -the person who extends Credit or lends money.

3. Free value of the note - the principal or amount borrowed.

4. Data of the note - the date the note is made or signed.

5. Maturity date - the due date of the note.

6. Term of the note - the length of time covered by the note.

A promissory note may be transferred from one person to another. In transferring the note, the holder endorses it, and perfects the transfer by delivery. A note that is transferred and accepted by another person is called a negotiable promissory note.

A non-interest bearing promissory note is basically the same in appearance with an interest-bearing note, except that it does not mention of any interest rate. Since no interest is imposed for the loan amount, the maturity value of a non-interest bearing note is equal to its principal.

Discounting of an Interest-bearing Promissory Note

Promissory notes arise because of credit. Usually, business entities, banks, and persons-in order to increase their sales or Output-extend credit to customers or sale products and services on account. This type of transaction is usually supported by promissory notes.

Discounting of a promissory note refers to the selling of the note before its maturity date. It is one way for a business or creditor to finance its receivable. When a Promissory note is discounted, the payee sells the note to the bank and receives the proceeds at a discount. On the due date the bank receives the maturity value of the note, that is, the principal plus the interest.

The following procedures may be observed in discounting a promissory note:

1. Determine the maturity value of the note using the following formula:

Maturity Value = Principal [1 + (Rate x Time]

2. Determine the discount period. Discount period refers to the remaining period from the date of discounting up to the maturity date. In counting the remaining number of

days or discount period, always remember to exclude the first day but include the last day.

3. Determine the discount using the following formula:

Discount (D) = Maturity value (M) x Discount rate (d) x Discount period (t)

4. Determine the proceeds using the formula:

Proceeds (W) = Maturity value (M) - Discount (D)

Discounting of a Non-interest Bearing Promissory Note

When a non-interest bearing note is discounted, the maturity value is equal to its principal. In other words, there 18 no need to compute for the maturity value; hence, the procedures are less than 1 step from that of discounting an interest-bearing note.

Relationships between Interest Rate and Discount Rate

In discounting promissory notes, there are two types of interests that are used, namely the interest rate and the discount rate.

The interest rate is the rate that appears on the promissory note; the discount rate is the rate used by the bank or the buyer of the promissory notes. It is emphasized that interest rate is different from discount rate. In case, however; that no discount rate is provided, the interest rate is assumed to be the discount rate.

Another difference between the two is that the interest rate is used to compute the maturity value of the promissory note. The maturity value is the full amount that the borrower will pay on the due date. On the other hand, the discount rate is used to determine the discount and proceeds of the discounting.

However, there is a similarity or direct relation between the interest rate and the discount rate on either their future values or present values. In the succeeding discussion, we will evaluate their relationship based on present values.

Let us recall first the present value (the value now) formulas of simple interest and simple discount. The formula to compute the present value of an amount at simple interest is:

$$P = \frac{M}{(1+RT)}$$

where:

P = Principal

M = Maturity value
R = Interest rate
T = Time

On the other hand, the formula to determine the present value of a discount is:

D = M (1 - dT)

where:
D = Discount
M = Maturity value
d = Discount rate
T = Time

Effective Rate of Interest

Effective rate of interest refers to the true or real interest. It is measured based on the ratio of interest or discount over the sum of the proceeds of the borrowings and their terms.

In a simple interest note, the nominal rate is likewise considered as the true or effective interest, since the borrower receives the full amount of borrowings. In other words, the proceeds of the loan are equal to the principal.

Whereas in a discounted interest note, the borrower receives only the proceeds, that is, the difference between the maturity value and the discount. The proceeds are basically lower than the face value; hence, the interest in a discounted note is not the true or effective interest rate.

The formulas to compute the effective interest rate are as follows:

For simple interest note:

$$\text{Effective interest rate} = \frac{\text{Interest}}{\text{Principal} \times \text{Time}}$$

For discounted interest note:

$$\text{Effective interest rate} = \frac{\text{Discount}}{\text{Proceeds} \times \text{Time}}$$

Partial Payment of Notes

A simple interest promissory note is sometimes settled by the maker or holder through a series of partial payments instead of a single payment upon reaching the maturity date. In other words, the whole amount due (maturity value) is settled by a series of payments up to the due date.

Usually, the problem encountered in this case is the determination of the required payment to settle the whole obligation on the due date.

PART THREE

Compound Interest

Nature of compound Interest

In Part One, the concept of simple interest was discussed. It is called simple interest because the interest is computed only once during the terms of the loan or investment, or the interest is only earned based on the original investment or principal amount.

Compound interest

refers to the sum of interests of prior periods computed on the original or principal amount and each of successive periods on both the principal. In computing, compound interest for the first period, it is based on the principal and interest.

In computing compound interest for the first period, it is based on the principal. The interest due is then added to the principal for the next period, and the sum, which serves as the new principal, is the basis for the next interest computation. This process of adding the interest due to the new principal in succeeding periods continues until the due date. It is known as compounding of interest. Compound interest is also the difference between the original or principal amount-and the compound amount. The sum of the principal and all accumulated interests at the end of the term is the compound amount.

Terms Related to Compounding of Interest

In the computation of a compound interest, the following terms should be familiarized;

Nominal rate refers to the rate of borrowing and is usually quoted as an annual interest rate, unless otherwise specified. Frequency or number of conversions refers to the number of times the interest is added to the principal in a year. The frequency of conversion in a year may bimonthly, quarterly, semi-annually, or annually. The number of conversion periods during a loan term is also known as the compounding period.

Thus, a loan with a term of 2 years will have the following total compounding periods:

Period	Frequency	Term of the Loan	Total Compounding Periods
Annually.	1	2 years	2
Semi-annually	2	2 years	4
Quarterly.	4	2 years	8
Monthly.	12	2 years	24

The total number of conversion periods is the product of the frequency of conversion and the term of the loan.

Thus, a loan payable after 5 years term with quarterly frequency conversion has a total compounding period of 20.

Periodic rate or interest rate per compounding period refers to the interest rate per conversion period. It is equal to the nominal rate divided by the compounding period in a year.

Compound Amount

Compound amount is the accumulated value of the principal and all interest amounts of prior periods. In other words, it is the sum of the principal and all compound interest.

In determining the compound amount, the sum of the interest and the principal will be the basis for computing the interest of the next compounding period.

The process of adding the interest to the principal in computing for the interest of the next succeeding period continues up to the due date.

Compound Amount Formula

In the computation of compound interest, the total number of compounding period determines the frequency of computing the new interest and adding it to the running principal.

To simplify the voluminous computation when numerous compounding periods are involved, the above equation may be expressed as follows:

Compound amount $(C) = P(1+i)^n$

where:

C = Compound amount

P = Principal or present value

i = Periodic interest rate

n = Total number of compounding periods

The formula is used to compute the compound or future amount, if the interest is compounded.

Compound Amount with Fractional Interest Period

There are instances when the total number of compounding periods is not an integer but a fraction. This happens when the term does not coincide with the compounding periods or frequency of conversion.

For example, the term of the loan is 5 years and 2 months compounded quarterly.

The total compounding periods will be 20 2/3, computed as follows:

Compounding period = 4 (5212)

= 20 2/3

There are two methods of finding the compound amount with fractional interest period:
1. Direct substitution method
2. Practical method

In direct method, the compound amount is determined by directly substituting the given values to the compound amount formula.

The practical method, on the other hand, determines the compound amount by using two interest rates-the compound interest for the integer and the simple interest for the fraction.

Alternative Procedure for Practical Method

Another way of determining the compound amount with fractional period using the practical method is to compute the compound amount with an integer. The result, which is the new principal, will be the basis to compute the compound interest of the fraction using simple interest formula. The sum is the final compound amount.

Compound Amount at Varying Rates

Both creditor and debtor may agree to change the interest rate during the term of borrowing, if the debtor settles the obligation before the due date or requests for extension of borrowing terms. Similarly, the interest rates on bank deposits or investments may vary because of changes on previously agreed terms or implementation of a new monetary policy.

Under this particular situation, the compound amount at varying rates will be different from the compound amount computed at fixed interest rates.

The basic procedure under this case is to compute individually the compound amounts within particular terms. The new principal will be the basis in determining the compound amount of the succeeding period with different terms and interest.

Present Value of a Compound Amount

The concept of compound amount focuses on the determination of the future value of the principal. It answers the query: What is the value of the amount in the future if the interest is compounded?

The concept of present value, on the other hand, is directly opposite to the nature and attributes of a compound amount. It basically determines the value now or the amount of money worth today.

The present value of a compound amount is its discounted value. It is the principal of the compound amount. Although it is not the concern of this book to derive the formula, let us briefly discuss the derivation to see the relationship of the two formulas and have a deeper understanding of compound amount and present value.

The formula of the present value of compound amount is:
$P = C(1+i)^{-n}$

On the other hand, the formula of compound amount is expressed as
$C = P(1+i)^n$

where:
P = Principal or present value
C = Compound amount or future value
1 = Periodic interest rate
n = Total number of compounding period

By inspection, the opposite relation of the compound amount and present value formulas is noticeable. The formula of present value is basically derived from the formula of the compound amount.

Present Value with Fractional Interest Period

Sometimes, the terms of the borrowings or investment does not coincide with the compound period or the frequency of conversion. In such cases, the n of the discount factor is a combination of an integer and a fraction.

The applicable procedures in this situation slightly differ from that of finding the compound amount with fractional interest period discussed previously. But there are two methods in determining the present value of a compound amount with fractional interest periods. These are:

1. Direct substitution method
2. Practical method

Under the direct substitution method, the given data are directly substituted to the formula.

The practical method of discounting compound amount, on the other hand, uses the discount factor of the next higher integer. The total conversion periods will be deducted from the next higher integer, and the difference will be used as the interest period using simple interest.

The result of simple interest computation present value is based on the integer to determine the final present value.

For example, if the total conversion period is 23 1/3, the discount factor of the next higher integer, which is 24, will be used. The difference between 24 and 23 1/3, which is 2/3, will be computed based on simple interest. The final present value is equal to the sum of the present value of 24 conversion periods and the simple interest of 2/3 time period.

Finding the Interest Rate

Similar to the situation of simple interest, there are instances where the interest rate is not provided for a certain amount to be compounded for a given period of time. In other words, the nominal interest rate is unknown in the problem, while other values needed to compute for the compound amount in a future date are expressly given.

The computation in finding the interest rate centers on the basic formula compound amount where the factor $(1 + i)^n$ is an element.

The variable i in the factor $(1 + i)^n$ is the periodic interest rate. It is computed by dividing the nominal rate by the compounding periods. To compute for the nominal rate, the periodic rate is simply multiplied to the compounding periods. Hence:

Nominal rate (r) = Periodic rate (i) x Compounding period (n)

The nominal interest rate may be determined using the following methods:
1. Logarithmic method
2. Exponential method
3. Interpolation method

It is beyond the scope of this book to derive the formula; only the final formula is provided.

Logarithmic Method

The logarithmic method uses the table of logarithmic values.

To find i, the formula is:

1 = antilog(logC-logP/n)-1

where:

C = Compound amount or future amount

P = Principal or present value

n = Total number of compounding periods

Once the value of i has been computed, it is multiplied to the compounding period or the frequency of conversion to determine the nominal rate

Hence, to compute the nominal rate:

r = i (f)

r = i)
(
f

where:

r = Nominal rate

1 = Periodic interest rate

f = Compounding period or frequency of conversion

Exponential Method

To solve for i using the exponential method, the formula is:

$i = (C/P)^{1/n} - 1$

where:

C = Compound amount or future amount

P. = Principal or present value

n = Total number of compounding periods

Interpolation Method

The interpolation method makes use of the table of accumulated or compound values as a reference to determine the periodic interest rate.

The total number of compounding periods determines the value of n or the period column. In determining the reference value, the compound or future amount is divided by the principal. The result of such is equal to the compound value of P1, and the corresponding column where it falls determines the applicable interest rate.

In case the reference value is not equal to the compound values of P1 on the table of compound values, the difference is determined by the process of interpolation by taking the higher and lower figures.

This book adopts the exponential method to determine the periodic interest i.

Finding the Time

Sometimes, the length of time for a given principal or present value to accumulate in the future at a given interest rate is missing. In other words the term of the borrowings or investment of the compound amount formula is unknown.

The unknown terms or time may be computed using the
1. Logarithmic method
2. Interpolation method

This book uses the logarithmic method to solve for the missing terms or time.

Logarithmic Method
The number of compounding periods is computed from the basic formula of compound amount $C = P(1+i)^n$. From the process of derivation, the formula to compute for compounding periods is:

$n = (\log C - \log P)/(\log (1+i))$

Or

$n = (\log C/P)/(\log(1+i))$

Where:

n = Total number of compounding periods

C = Compound or future amount

P = Principal or present value

f = frequency of conversion

Since n in the discount factor $(1 + i)^n$ is computed by multiplying the terms with the frequency of conversions, the time is determined by reversing the process. Thus to determine the term or time, the total number of conversion periods n is divided by the frequency of conversion.

The formula to determine the time would be:

Time (T) = Number of conversion period (n) / Frequency of conversion (f)

T can be directly computed using the following formula:

$T = (\log C - \log P) / (f \log (1+i))$

Where:

n = Total number of compounding periods

C = Compound or future amount

P = Principal or present value

f = frequency of conversion

i = Periodic interest rate

T = Time of term

Relationship between Nominal and Effective Rates

In Part Two, the concept of effective rate is briefly discussed. Effective rate is the real or true interest rate of the borrowings or investments. It is a rate with a conversion period of 1 year. Effective rate is a special kind of nominal rate.

Nominal rate generally refers to rates appearing on the face of borrowing notes or the benchmark of an investment decision. It is an interest rate where the frequency of conversion can be more than 1 year. When the conversion period is 1 year, the nominal rate is also equal to the effective rate.

A nominal rate, therefore, is equal to its effective rate when the frequency of is 1 year or they produce equal amounts of interest on the same principal in the same length of time.

We also discussed in Part Two the relationship between simple interest rate and discount rate. We have learned that both rates are considered equal if they have the same present values at the same period of time, or if they give equal compound amounts at the end of the same period.

In this section, we will study the relationship of nominal and effective rates, Both rates, nominal and effective, are considered equal if they produce equal compound amounts at the end of the same period.

Relationship of Two Nominal Rates with Different Compounding Periods

A nominal rate with a certain compounding period may be equal to another nominal rate with a different compounding period at the end of the same term. The two nominal rates are only equal if they produce equal compound amounts in the same period of time.

Equation of Values

We learned in previous discussions that the value of an amount changes because of the following factors:

1. Terms
2. Interest rate
3. Conversion period

Likewise, we studied that a certain interest rate is equivalent to another interest rate for the same period of time. Similarly, the sum of one set of values is equal to the sum of another set of values on the same comparison date. The date where the two set of values are equal is called the focal date.

Focal Date

Focal date or comparison date refers to the point where the sum of one set of values is equal to the sum of another set of values, it is chosen arbitrarily. The use of focal point facilitates solving a problem which involves a set of new payments that settle the old obligations equated with each other.

Since the focal point is arbitrarily chosen, there is a possibility that one will have a different focal point from another. However, the answer that satisfies the requirement of the problem will still be the same.

BONUS KNOWLEDGE

What is Annuity?

Annuity refers to a sequence or series of equal payments made at an equal interval of time.

The definition identifies the elements of annuity as follows:

1. Sequence or series of payments
2. Payments are equal of amount
3. Made at an equal interval of time

Impliedly, if one of the elements is missing, the payment is not considered as an annuity. Similarly, a series of payments of equal amount but made not of equal interval of time is also not considered an annuity. Similarly, a series of payments of unequal amounts, though made at an equal interval of time, is not classified as an annuity.

The concept of annuity applies on premiums of life insurance, perio on rentals, purchase of cars or houses, interest payment on bonds or payments on household appliances purchased on instalment.

Kinds of Annuities

1. Annuity certain - It is an annuity with definite term. The first and last payment intervals have definite dates. Payments on installment of household appliances are annuity certain.

2. Annuity uncertain - It is an annuity with an indefinite term. The first payment interval has a definite date, but the last payment interval cannot be determined.

3. Ordinary annuity- It is an annuity where periodic payments are made at the end of the payment interval.

4. Annuity due - It is an annuity where the periodic payments are made at the beginning of the payment interval.

5. Deferred annuity- It is an annuity where the first periodic payment begins other than the first payment interval.

6. Simple annuity - It is an annuity where payment intervals coincide with the interest compounding period.

7. Complex annuity - It is an annuity where payment intervals do not coincide with the interest compounding period.

At the end of this book, you should be able to:

From Part One

a. Discuss the nature of interest;

b. Identify the parties in transactions involving payment of interest;

c. Identify the elements in computing interest;

d. Describe the concept of simple interest;

e. Find interest, principal, rate, and time if unknown;

f. Discuss the concept of maturity value;

g. Differentiate ordinary from exact interest method;

h. Describe the relationship between ordinary and exact interest;

i. Determine exact time and approximate time;

j. Identify the four combinations of computing interest when time given is between interest rates; and

k. Describe the procedures in convening time expressed in decimal into days.

From Part Two

a. Describe the nature of discount;

b. Discuss the phrase "to discount;"

c. Discuss the concept of present value;

d. Describe the nature of bank discount;

e. Determine the amount or size of loan to be discounted;

f. Identify the types of promissory notes;

g.   Identify the parts of a promissory note;

h.   Determine proceeds of discounted interest-bearing and non-interest bearing notes;

i.   Discuss the relation between interest rate and discount rate;

j.   Determine effective interest rate;

k.   And identify the amount due on notes with a series of partial payments.

From Part Three

a.   Describe the nature of compound interest;

b.   Define the terms related to compound interest computation;

c.   Discuss how a compound amount is computed;

d.   Compute the present value of a compound amount;

e.   Determine unknown values using different methods;

f.   Identify the relationship between nominal and effective interest rate;

g.   Discuss the concept of continuous compounding; and

h.   Discuss the nature of equation of values.

www.ingramcontent.com/pod-product-compliance
Lightning Source LLC
Chambersburg PA
CBHW030051230526
45471CB00003B/1044